CW00566787

Like Dreams & Clouds

EMPTINESS & INTERDEPENDENCE
MAHAMUDRA & DZOGCHEN

Ringu Tulku Rinpoche

Bodhicharya
PUBLICATIONS
Awaken the heart by opening the mind

First Published in 2011 by
BODHICHARYA PUBLICATIONS
24 Chester Street, Oxford, OX4 1SN, United Kingdom.
www.bodhicharya.org   email: publications@bodhicharya.com

Printed on recycled paper by Imprint Digital, Devon, UK.

ISBN 978-0-9534489-8-2
Second Edition. 2013

Emptiness and Interdependence: transcript and editing by Mary Heneghan and Jonathan Clewley

Mahamudra and Dzogchen: transcript and first edit by Corinne Segars.
Second edit by Margaret Ford and Pat Little

Bodhicharya Publications team, for this book: Tim Barrow; Annie Dibble; Marita
Faaberg; Margaret Ford; Mary Heneghan; Eric Masterton; Rachel Moffitt; Jet Mort;
Pat Murphy; Paul O'Connor; Minna Stenroos; Claire Trueman; David Tuffield.

Typesetting & Design by Paul O'Connor at www.judodesign.com
Cover Image: *'Rainbow in Sikkim'* courtesy of Andries Pelser.

THE HEART WISDOM SERIES
BY RINGU TULKU RINPOCHE

No. 1 - Mahamudra & Dzogchen
[reprinted in Heart Wisdom No. 4]

No. 2 - The Ngöndro
Foundation Practices of Mahamudra

No. 3 - From Milk to Yoghurt
A Recipe for Living and Dying

No. 4 - Like Dreams and Clouds
Emptiness and Interdependence; Mahamudra and Dzogchen

No. 5 - Dealing with Emotions
Scattering the Clouds

No. 6 - The Journey from Head to Heart
Along a Buddhist Path

Like stars, mists and candle flames;
Mirages, dew-drops and water bubbles;
Like dreams, lightning and clouds;
In that way, I will view all composite phenomena.

Wishing Prayer
Kagyu Monlam Prayer Book

Contents

Editors' Preface

Emptiness or Interdependence describes the key philosophical view of Buddhism. An experiential understanding of this is the basis for a true appreciation of Buddhist teaching. In this way, we hope what is presented here offers something for a wide range of new students and experienced practitioners. Ringu Tulku gives us a short, clear, step-by-step practical discussion of this central topic and looks at how it applies to our lives. At the same time, he points us towards the great mystery that opens out as our understanding deepens.

This teaching is combined here with another teaching by Ringu Tulku which was originally published as the first in the Heart Wisdom series. This covers Mahamudra and Dzogchen, approaches which provide skilful means and an overall path by which we can realise the true nature of ourselves, our world and all things - as none other than emptiness or interdependence.

With very great thanks to Ringu Tulku for bringing these timeless teachings through to us with their subtleties and depth, in a way we can understand and use.

May all beings be happy and peaceful and come to know things just as they are.

Mary Heneghan and Jonathan Clewley
For Bodhicharya Publications

Emptiness & Interdependence

THE BUDDHIST VIEW OF HOW THINGS EXIST

Ringu Tulku Rinpoche

The Abbey, Sutton Courtenay, Oxfordshire
29th April 2010

Emptiness & Interdependence

What is this?

The concept of Emptiness, or Interdependence, is the main philosophy of Buddhism, especially Mahayana Buddhism. There are many detailed discussions of this important topic, looking at it from all sides and with different approaches. There are the Prajnaparamita Sutras, for example, which are all on this subject. So we could spend a long time debating, asking questions, using logic and analysis to go deeper and look to see if there is a contradiction between the way we generally perceive things and the results of intellectual analysis of how things are. But here we are going to look at this topic in a short way, in a direct and concise way.

Many different terms are used for this concept. They are all trying to get at the same thing. You can say Emptiness or Interdependence or Co-dependent Arising or Co-dependent Origination. People also use terms such as 'voidness' or 'absence' or 'openness'. In Sanskrit it is *shunyata*. But whatever term you use, whether interdependence, or *shunyata* (usually translated as 'emptiness'), they are all exactly one and the same. This is something very important to understand.

Nagarjuna said: 'Because there is nothing that is not dependently arising, therefore there is nothing that is not emptiness in nature'. That is the understanding. Interdependence or dependent arising is about the way any phenomenon, any 'thing', *is*. It is about the viewpoint— any analytical or logical way of experimenting with, and asking, this question for yourself. Look at anything, whether it is a material thing or a person or an event or the mind, whatever, and say: 'What is this? What is the way this exists? Does it exist as a completely independent thing? Or is it dependent on other things?' If it is something existing totally independently, then, because it is independent, the existence of it should not depend on anything else.

The existence of *this* [meditation gong stick] cannot be independent because it is made up of many causes and conditions. Many, many causes and conditions inter-relate to create this gong stick as it is now. At one level we can see the wood it is made of came from a tree which itself was dependent on many causes and conditions to grow. The stick is also made up of many elements. And it is changing, maybe slowly, but it does not remain the same year after year. If the stick was actually 'one' thing and was unchanging, then we could say that it was totally independent. But we can see it is not 'one'. It is made up of many parts, many elements, many causes and conditions. It cannot be independent because it is made up of many elements.

This is exactly what we mean by dependent arising: whatever thing, whether it is a huge thing like a universe, or a minute thing like a part of an atom, everything exists dependently. Everything is made up of many elements and causes and conditions, and everything changes.

Right and left

When you say interdependent or dependently arising, it does not mean only: 'this is one thing and this is another thing, and these two are dependent on each other'. It is not like that, but more like: '*this*' cannot exist without '*this*'. One example can be '*right*' and '*left*'. Right and left totally depend on each other. So when there is no right, there is no left; and when there is no left there is no right. Almost in this way, everything that is there, any object, anything that we think about, all these things are made up of many things. 'Many' means that when all of these conditions come together then that thing seems to be there. But each of these things, each of these elements, is dependent on many things and each of these elements that make up one of them is *also* many things. So if you ask whether you can really find something that is totally *one*, it may be difficult to find something that is one.

One or many?

There are lots of dialogues, lots of questions, lots of reasoning and logic trying to find the nature of things. One very important question that is asked is: 'Is it *one* or *many*?' You can look at anything and ask, 'Is it one or many?' If it is one, then it has to be something totally indivisible and totally unaffected by anything. And it has to be something that exists on its own without changing, because if it changes other elements are affecting it. Changing means some elements are getting away and some elements are getting in, that is what changing means. So if it changes, then it cannot be independent, because changing is a process. If changing takes place, that means something that was there before is not there now. Something that was not there before comes in, and therefore things change.

Is there anything that cannot change? That is the question. Is there anything that is totally independent, which is totally *one*, which is not affected by anything, which does not change? If that condition is there, then you say this is *one*. But it is very difficult to find something like that, except in theory. We cannot say anything is totally *one*.

If you cannot say there is totally *one*, then although you may say that everything is made up of many things, because there are many elements and many conditions and many causes, you cannot find *many* because *many* would have to be made up of *many* 'one's. So, therefore, from the Buddhist point of view the whole of phenomena is neither *one* nor *many*. You cannot find one because you cannot find a totally existing *one* thing, independent. And because you cannot find one thing totally existent and unaffected by anything, therefore even the tiniest building block that makes things up, has to be *something*. If it is some*thing* then it has to be something that can be affected, that can change, that can be divided. If it is no*thing*, then it is not.

Magical existence

It is very difficult to find one *thing*. Since there is no one, which could be the building block of everything, everything exists in a very magical way. That is the Buddhist way of understanding: things are interdependent, dependently arising. There is nothing existing totally on its own, but still everything exists. And that way of existing can only be explained as dependently arising, dependently existing. And in this way of being, way of existing, since you cannot find anything that is existing totally on its own, therefore we say its nature is emptiness.

The nature of things is emptiness

Emptiness does not mean there is nothing. Emptiness means the way everything *is* — the way everything manifests, the way everything appears — is interdependently manifesting. But there is no one totally independent thing. So, therefore, the nature of things is emptiness. And because this nature is emptiness, it is possible to manifest in all different kinds of ways; and it is possible to grow; and it is possible to live; and it is possible to produce. If it were something totally independent and existing on its own, this growing and changing and manifesting and living would not be possible. Because growing and changing and living, all these kinds of 'chemistries', all the beautiful manifestations of the world, have to be very flexible, very affected by causes and conditions. Things have lots of causes and conditions and each cause and condition makes the whole thing in a very different way. And it can change its course, its way, its colour, and all its different aspects. And that is because the nature of things is emptiness.

The possibility of transformation

This is the basis of the Buddhist view of reality: the reality of every phenomenon, whether it is yourself or anything else. Because of this, causes and conditions become very important. From the Buddhist point of view, this is not just an intellectual understanding. It is not just an intellectual way of seeing how things might be. There is an important reason to look into this — *the way that things are* — and that is because people, beings, don't want to suffer. They don't want pain and problems. They don't want dissatisfaction. They want to be satisfied and fearless and happy. Now, even pain and problems and suffering have their causes and conditions, and because of certain causes and conditions then there is more suffering. But even this suffering, this problematic situation, this way of being in a problematic situation, is not something unchangeable. Because it is something that has arisen out of causes and conditions. It is something impermanent, something interdependent and dependently arising.

So, therefore, if you change some elements out of a situation; if you change a certain way of looking at it, or if certain causes and conditions change, then the whole situation can change. So there is the possibility for everything to transform. Everything can be changed. This philosophy of interdependence and emptiness gives the philosophical background for this possibility of transformation.

Emptiness is not nothingness

The understanding of emptiness is not nihilistic. It is always said to be very important that 'emptiness' is not seen as 'nothingness'. The understanding is not a nihilistic view that nothing matters because everything is non-existent. Instead, it is very important to see the causes and conditions of things.

Karma: causes and conditions

The more we understand the nature of interdependence and emptiness, the more we understand the importance of causes and conditions: The importance of each element, the importance of each action, the way we see things, the way we react, the way we act, for ourselves and for others as well. So, therefore, this is a very important understanding from the Buddhist point of view, that these two things have to come together: the understanding of interdependence and emptiness has to come together with the understanding of what we call karma, or causes and conditions. And this also has to come together with the understanding of transformation. The philosophy of Buddhism is these two things together: *interdependence-emptiness* and *karma-transformation*.

Everything can change

What I do, how I think, how I act, what kind of habitual tendencies I have—all this is something that is not concrete, not solid, not something existing on its own. Even *me*, what I think, my personality, my habits, the way my emotions work—all these things are not something totally solid and existing on their own that cannot be changed. It is nothing like that. Everything can be changed because there is nothing that is not dependently arising. Because everything is not independent, everything is dependent. If one element, one cause, one condition can change, everything can change. That even applies to our emotions, for instance; how we react. If I feel a certain emotion like sadness, anger, fear, or have any kind of negative or problematic situation, this is also because of many causes and conditions. If I can work on one element, and change that, the way I experience will change.

Understanding emptiness is not just theoretical

It is important to say that the understanding of interdependence and emptiness is not just intellectual or theoretical. It is not just something that philosophers and intellectuals can debate upon. They write theses and they write papers but if nothing happens in their way of being— then it is just intellectual and theoretical and does not serve the purpose of why we study. The study and understanding of interdependence and emptiness have to serve the purpose of transforming ourselves, so that our way of experiencing ourselves can change. The important thing is that, through understanding and experience of the way I understand phenomena—how things are, how I am—through that, it can become a way of transforming myself by learning what I am, and how things are, and how I experience things. Through that, I can actually learn how to experience things better; how to deal with my emotions; how to deal with my problems and situations and reactions—so that I become wiser. Wiser, in the sense that I know how to deal with any situation: I can become more peaceful, happier; have fewer problems and fewer painful situations.

Emotions: the three conditions of anger

When you look into the nature of things, it is not to understand them in an intellectual way, but to 'see' experientially. When we talk about 'the view' in Buddhism it is not just a philosophy. It is more like the way I react and understand and experience things. Look at an emotion, for instance, because an emotion is an important part of our life. If I were able to deal with my emotions then I would be able to deal with any situation. In Buddhism this becomes the most important issue: how to deal with our emotions, and so we talk a lot about this.

Anger is often used as an example in many teachings for understanding and discussion because, of all the negative emotions and kleshas, anger is seen as the most destructive. Other emotions are sometimes okay, sometimes positive, sometimes more negative; sometimes they bring the basis of problems. So, therefore, it is important to deal with them, but it is not an emergency. Anger is said to be more of an emergency, because with anger and hatred, if you act on them, they can bring a very strong and immediate problem to yourself and others. So often we take anger as an example.

The first condition: the root

To have a very strong emotion like anger (or anything else, this is just one example) there are three reasons, three main conditions. One is what we call the root: we are still confused, we do not see things completely clearly, we do not understand the nature of ourselves, we do not see everything, how things really are. We are not enlightened; that is one cause—the root. We have the seed of anger, the seed of our kleshas. If that is not there, then the emotion would not happen—there is no seed. But we all have this seed.

The second condition: the object

The second condition is that there is something happening. There is an object or a situation that makes you angry. Either somebody does something bad, or says something bad, or something happens that makes you angry and unhappy. Something happens, which is the object of the negative emotion. That is the second condition.

The third condition: the way of looking

Then the third condition is that you have a wrong way of looking at the situation. You take it in a negative way, not in a positive way. The way in which you look at the situation is what makes you angry. So when you have these three conditions together, you get upset, you get angry. You can become hateful and then you can act in a very aggressive and harmful way towards others, which is also harmful to yourself.

The first two conditions, the root and the object, are very difficult to change. Until you are totally free from any kleshas, you cannot change the first condition, the root. It is there. The second condition is also very difficult to change because you cannot get rid of all the things around you or in the world that make you upset. You cannot take away all the problematic situations, all the bad people, all the negative actions. You cannot get rid of them, so therefore they are always there. The third condition is the only thing we can change—the way we look; the way we react.

This is one of the main things: if I can understand that it would not be useful to react with anger and aggression, because that will make me suffer and everybody suffer, I cannot react like that. I have to react in a different way, I have to act with more patience; with more understanding; with more wisdom; so that I suffer less, and I create fewer problems for everybody. When that understanding becomes real then that emotion does not arise in that way.

I am changing phenomena

In this way, I see that things are very interdependent and are dependently arising. Their nature is emptiness. I am not one thing; I am also changing phenomena. I am not an independent thing. I am a dependently arising thing. I am changing all the time. There is not one moment in which I am not changing. All my experiences and all my thoughts and emotions are arising out of this. In *this* moment, I have my thoughts and emotions arising. And in the *next* moment, another thought and emotion is arising. They are continuously arising. This emotion that I have here now is gone in the next moment and another is arising. When I understand the way *I am*, the way my emotions work, the way everything is dependently arising, I see there is no one thing that is very concrete. And I, also, am a continuously changing phenomenon. I am not only one thing. I am changing all the time.

We see impermanence as remote

This is also a very important part of the understanding of emptiness: impermanence. Everybody knows that things change, nothing is permanent, but we don't see *how much* it is changing. We say things change. But how much do they change? Do things change once a year? Or do they change once a day? Or do they change once a minute, or once a second, or more than that? We usually think that changing means *now*: change, *now*: not change. But if you look deeply, when is the time things do not change? When is the time that time does not change, things do not change, I do not change? When you cannot find a time when things do not change, then when is the time that things exist on their own?

I am like a river

There is no time that things exist on their own. There is no time that things do not change. Because of this, everything is like a process; it is fluid; it is like a river. The example that is often given is '*me*'. We say '*I am*': I am a person, I am a being, I am one thing, I am an individual. But actually you can say it is a little bit like a river. When you look at the river, it is one river. It was there yesterday. It was there the day before. It was there last year. It has been there for thousands of years. But is it the same river? It is flowing in the same direction. It is the same kind of body of water. But the water that flows there *now* is not there ...*now*. It is totally different water. The water of yesterday, or even the water of the last moment, is not the same as the water of the next moment.

In a similar way, I am changing all the time. And yet it is not really that *I* am changing all the time: *everything* is changing all the time. And, therefore, where is the *I* in this? When we understand that everything is like that, then what is there to hold on to? There is nothing to hold on to. There is nothing that we can really hold on to. So every thought, every emotion, every reaction, every experience, everything that happens, we have to let happen; we have to let go.

No need to struggle

So, then, what is the use of fear? There is nothing to fear, because if it is changing so much, it is always flowing. There is nothing you can hold on to because it is not possible to hold on to anything; it is *always* changing. There is nothing that you can protect. There is nothing you can secure. But, because there is nothing you can secure, there is also nothing that can be destroyed, because it is always changing anyway. When it is always changing, what is there to be destroyed?

There is nothing to be destroyed in me because everything that is in 'me' is constantly changing phenomena— my body is a constantly changing phenomenon, my mind is a constantly changing phenomenon. There is nothing that is here independently. So, when one understands that that is the case, what is it that I am so afraid of? There is nothing that can be totally secured, but there is nothing that can be destroyed because there is nothing that can be secured. The more I understand that, the more I understand *anatman*, 'selflessness'. It is not a concept of denying myself, saying 'I am not here.' Selflessness is not that. The more deeply we understand, the more we understand that selflessness is knowing that what I experience is a fleeting thing. There is nothing which can protect it but there is nothing which can be totally destroyed, because it is a flowing, it is a process.

This moment of experience......this moment of experience......this moment of experience........is the reality. When I understand this, there is no need to carry the burden of the past. No need to fear or panic too much about what will happen in the future. It is possible to be totally absorbed in the present moment and enjoy the beauty of the present. Because you can do that you can be one hundred percent alive at this very moment. You can be clear about this moment and understand there is no need to struggle. There is no need to struggle because there is nothing to struggle for. The struggle does not work.

Peace of mind

When that understanding happens, then peace of mind comes naturally— because you understand what you are. You understand how to deal with your thoughts and emotions and habitual tendencies, because you see the way we have been working and reacting all along has been with a very intense struggle. An intense kind of tension: always trying to run against *the* current; to hold on to things that are impossible to hold on to; to fight things that are impossible to fight; to try to secure things that are impossible to secure. And afraid of things that we need not be afraid of. When that understanding happens, then we can totally relax. And that is the greatest relief and peace; we call it stability. And sometimes we call it inner realisation. Because through that realisation, the more you understand emptiness and interdependence (whether you call it selflessness or *Self*), the more you know how to deal with your problems and your habitual tendencies.

Paramita: transcending habitual tendencies

This is the main message of the Buddha, the main teaching of this practice or philosophy. Everything in Buddhism is actually somehow leading to this understanding. Every practice, every step, all the teachings, everything is leading to this, because this is what is called wisdom. Then any thing we do with that understanding or experience, with that attitude, any work we do, any training we do, becomes what we call *'paramita'*. It becomes a way to totally transcend our usual habitual tendencies, and become enlightened.

If we change our usual habitual tendencies, or our usual ways of working, a little bit, with the wisdom that comes from understanding emptiness, it becomes *paramita*. For example, becoming more generous, working on generosity; or trying to live with good conduct; or trying to work on any kind of positive way of acting— helping other beings, meditation and things like that. This training has its own very strong importance because how we do things and how we react to things is what becomes important.

It is not that emptiness is understood and then there are no more problems, everything is perfect. It is not like that. Emptiness and inter-dependence mean that karma is important. My action is important. My reaction is important because things are interdependent. Anything that I do has its effect: an effect on myself and an effect on others. It is not that there is no effect because everything is emptiness.

So, the understanding is emptiness and karma together, as I have already said. But it is very important that understanding emptiness makes us more conscious of the effect of our actions, not otherwise. The more we understand emptiness and the interdependent nature of things, the more we become careful about, and aware of, the effect of our actions and reactions. And so, therefore, the more positive we are. The Prajnaparamita Sutras are the teachings on this.

I was actually asked to go through the Prajnaparamita Sutra, the Heart Sutra. But I said it is complicated and too long to discuss in one evening. I said let us discuss something, whatever comes to my mind, and then include your discussion, so we would discuss from both sides. I meant not to talk too much actually, but to give a point to base our discussion on, and then throw it open to everybody to take part. So, you can ask questions or say anything you like. It's open.

Questions and discussion

Enlightened Mind

Student: Can I draw the conclusion from what you have been saying, that 'enlightened mind' is independent?

Rinpoche: What is 'enlightened mind'?

Student: Yes, that is a good question!

Rinpoche: When you say enlightened mind is independent or dependent, whatever, there is nothing called *'enlightened mind'* as some *'thing'*. You can say 'what is mind?' Mind is what? Dependent or independent? But you cannot say enlightened mind is dependent or independent because enlightened mind is the perception. It is not about a *'thing'*. It is a perception.

Student: Maybe it's the wrong word. What about *'enlightened nature'*?

Rinpoche: There's nothing called 'enlightened nature'. I think it is like this: The way that things are, is the way things are. If you want you can call it interdependence, or emptiness. That is one way of describing it. But it is *describing it*—the words are only symbols. There is not necessarily any meaning in the words themselves—because you can call anything 'emptiness'. There are people called 'Shunyata'. Words themselves do not mean it, but the understanding is that the way the nature *is*, is the way the nature *is*.

Now, what is enlightened or unenlightened mind? When you can experience or understand and live by the way that things are, that is the enlightened mind. And when you are deluded, when you do not understand things, when you are confused, that is the unenlightened mind. There is nothing called '*enlightened mind*' here. The mind is the same, enlightened or unenlightened. It is the same thing. The way I am is the way I am. But I can be very confused or I can be not confused.

Changelessness

Student: I think one can get the wrong impression from texts using this language about recognising the nature of mind as 'changeless', for example. It can lead to a misconception that once one has stripped away all the negative emotions it can lead to something that is perhaps 'pure' and 'unchanging'.

Rinpoche: It is like this: When you say things are interdependent and therefore there is nothing independently existing, and the nature of things is emptiness; that means that everything is unborn and unceasing. This is another thing which is in the Prajnaparamita Sutra: it says 'unborn, unceasing'. Now, when you say that everything is unborn and unceasing, what does that mean? It means, because there is nothing existing totally on its own, therefore, what is born? Nothing can be born, because it is not existing on its own. It is just like an illusion. It is like a kind of mirage. You cannot say when the mirage is born, because the mirage is not there. So, therefore, it is also non-ceasing, because there is nothing to die. Like Milarepa said in this very famous and important poem:

> '*I was afraid of death*
> *And then ran away into the mountains.*
> *There I meditated on the uncertainly of death,*
> *And I meditated so much on the uncertainty of death,*
> *That I found deathlessness.*
> *So now if death comes,*
> *I have no fear.*'

There are two things: In order to find deathlessness, he had to not *secure* himself, but to meditate on the uncertainty of death. When you understand and become very clear about the imminence of death, you see it is coming every moment, it is always there, things are always changing. You find that there is nothing called '*death*' because there is nothing called '*existing*': nothing existing as an independent thing. When that understanding comes, it is not like: '*Now I am ... so impermanent ... it's so impermanent ... I am always changing*'. It is not like that. When you understand impermanence deeply, clearly, then actually there is nothing called impermanence because it is the way *it is*. In a way, there is nothing to die and there is nothing called death. The experience you get from that point of view is '*deathlessness*'.

Sometimes it can be explained or experienced as '*changeless*'. It is still changing but there is nothing called '*change*'. So it is changeless—because there is no birth, no death, no arising, no cessation. In fact there is nothing there to be born. There is nothing there to die. So, therefore, there is nothing there to change. So there are these two things: the '*changeless nature*' and '*always changing*'. The different philosophers and great masters who all had different experiences, expressed this in different ways. Sometimes it is expressed as '*emptiness*' and sometimes it is expressed as '*changelessness*'. It comes to the same thing. It is talking about exactly the same thing, the same experience, just using different words.

Joining Wisdom with Compassion

Student: The teachings seem to emphasise trying to understand emptiness and at the same time trying to practice compassion, and bringing these two things together. Can you explain that a bit?

Rinpoche: That is exactly it. These do come together. They have to come together. That is the whole point—because the more you understand the nature of yourself, the way things are, the more you understand that there is nothing to grasp. '*Me*' and '*others*' are not two separate things. The less you become selfish or self-centred, the more you become compassionate—no? Because compassion here is your heart being open. The less you have to do something just thinking about yourself, the more you understand there is nothing to do for yourself actually. You have only compassion. Also, the more you understand that there is a possibility to transform and change your way of experiencing, the more deeply the compassion comes and the more it is optimistic. You can transform this painful and struggling samsaric state of mind, which is always either running away or running after things. You understand that everybody can and should be free from this suffering that is uselessly happening.

Sometimes our compassion is about looking at the suffering and then feeling bad about it. That is the first kind of compassion people understand: people having problems and pain and then we feel bad about that. That is one level of compassion. The second level of compassion, which is very much to do with the Buddhist way of thinking, is wanting to free beings from suffering. The Buddhist way of understanding compassion is about really wishing and wanting and trying to do something about how to be free from suffering. That is the second level.

But then the next level of compassion is that you really see that there is a possibility of this. There is a possibility to transform, a possibility to change—in yourself and then others also. When that happens then that kind of compassion becomes much more practical, much stronger and much clearer. That can only come if you have the wisdom, the understanding of the nature of things, whether you call this wisdom understanding emptiness or whatever you call it—interdependence, emptiness, the nature of the mind, or whatever. When that experience becomes clearer then the compassion becomes more experiential. It is no longer just: "I want to be compassionate". It becomes more natural.

This is the connection between wisdom and compassion. From the Buddhist point of view, the more wisdom you have (what we call wisdom, which is the understanding of the nature of things) the more compassion becomes normal and experiential. And the more real compassion you experience, actually the more wisdom it leads to. This is because compassion brings you out of your old way of experiencing, not in a conceptual way but experientially. The more you have the experience of not grasping at yourself, holding on to your own, the more clearly the wisdom can come. That is the general understanding.

Letting go and letting be

Student: You said there is nothing to strive for and nothing to be afraid of and yet this 'I' is something we do try to hold on to. Usually we hold it very dear and can't really let go of it. Can you say something about how to gradually loosen this grasping?

Rinpoche: That is the difficult part. That is why it is not enough to have this understanding at the intellectual level only. We need to bring it to the experiential level. That is why we say that the most difficult and the longest journey is from your head to your heart. So, therefore, I think it is not worth expecting things to change too quickly. It is not easy to change our habits and habitual tendencies just like that. As long as we have this samsaric way of reacting, we will have this experience. So we need to try to understand a little bit and then a little bit use this understanding on a moment-by-moment basis.

That is why mindfulness is important. As an experience comes up, whether it is a strong negative emotion, a strong aversion or a strong clinging; at that moment we need to bring our awareness to it. We need to see that this way of reacting is not giving me any real thing that is good. If I react in this way and keep on reacting in this way, it is neither going to give me any happiness nor is it good for anybody else. It does not help. It does not work. It does not solve any problems if I react like this. Instead, I need to let be.

So, therefore, I need to learn how to let my mind relax and divert my attention away from this strong negative reaction and let something else come in. This is very important. If I really knew deeply that every moment, every emotion or every reaction that is arising in me, is arising and then dissolving and arising and dissolving, then I could also be a little bit clearer that this too is something that is arising. This is an emotion that is arising. The next moment, another emotion can arise. The next moment, another. It is not so much about what is happening around me but more about how I am reacting to it.

At any moment you can have lots of things happening in your life or around you. You can have something really very bad happening, a difficult thing happening, but at the same time there is something very good happening also, a nice thing happening. And many other things happening also. But our mind is habituated to only hold on to the difficult things: "There is a problem, there is a problem. Unless I can get rid of this problem I cannot think about anything else. I cannot do anything else." That is our habit. Whether we like it or not, that is the way we are. And then we think, "If only this problem is solved, then I can relax. I can only relax then, not before." This problem might be solved or it might not be solved. Sometimes it is solved, sometimes it is not solved. But other problems certainly come along. So, even if it is solved or a little bit goes away, another problem comes, and then I hold onto that. When that goes away, another comes, and I hold onto that. Then, when in life do you have time to relax? There is no time to relax. And it becomes more and more like this.

It is necessary, it is very important—it is a '*must*'—that we learn not to only hold on to one thing but also to let other things come in. That does not mean that I totally deny a problem. I do not have to say: "This problem is not existing, there are only good things happening". This is not the case. I have to do whatever I can to solve this problem; that is okay. But I do not have to totally lock in on that and nothing else. If I can solve this problem, whatever I have to do, I have to do it. If there is nothing I can do, then there is nothing I can do. There is no use doing anything; I just have to let be. That does not mean that I cannot think and feel and focus my mind towards other things. Because how I feel is about where I focus my mind. If my mind is focused on something nice and positive and good, I already feel good. If my mind is focused on something difficult and problematic, my mind is already sad and unhappy. In one way, it is very easy to make yourself happier because you just have to focus on something nicer and the moment will change.

That is the practice, the practice of learning how to make your mind flexible. That is meditation. Meditation is nothing but training our mind to be more flexible, so that we are not only locked onto our habitual tendency of experiencing and focusing on problems, but can let our mind remain wherever we want to focus it. If I want to focus my mind on my breathing, it remains there. If I want to focus on something like compassion or kindness, my mind remains there. Just on that flower? - it remains there. So that is the training. That is the practice. We learn, we kind of exercise, so that our mind is not only focusing on habitual problematic situations but also on other things. And that is where to start.

Dreams

Student: What about dreaming? Does this training also extend to what happens when you are asleep?

Rinpoche: The Buddhist literature says that dreams can be of four kinds. One kind of dream is related to your habitual tendencies—what you usually do in the day or things that are influencing your mind in life, that come into your mind and then you dream about them. That is one kind of dream. Another kind of dream is said to be due to your humours—the balance of humours in your body and whether your health is up or down—these can influence different things to come up in your dreams. Sometimes you can have very strange dreams. They are not necessarily from your experience of your life, but something different. They are dreams coming from your humours, and are more related to your health.

Then there are dreams because of the way your mind travels through your channels, how your mind is in your different channels and different systems, like the nervous system. Because of that you can dream that you see totally different colours and things and places you have never seen before. This is another type of dream. And the fourth type of dream is said to be more intuitive. Because the nature of mind is clarity—there is a clarity that is the nature of the mind—and because of this it has the capacity to experience and see past, present and future. It can see future things, so there can be intuitive dreams where you see your future, like predictions. So these are the four kinds of dreams you can have.

Mostly, though, dreams are more like a test: how you would react. Because dreams are at a deeper level of consciousness than our waking level of consciousness, a little deeper than that, it is a deeper kind of habitual tendency. How you react in the dream is said to be an indication of how you might react when you are in Bardo, after you die. How you will react at that time would depend on that deep level of your consciousness. So, therefore, the way you react in the dream can be very significant because that could be the way you react after death. If at the dream level you are reacting very positively, very strongly and nicely and positively, that means that you are doing well. It is seen as a test of how deeply your practice goes and things like that.

That is the general way of seeing dreams from the Buddhist point of view. If you can meditate during the dream, if you can practice in the dream, if you can change your reactions at the dream level; that means you are doing very well. That is a stronger practice.

Student: I was thinking that you may wish in your waking life to be very compassionate but your dream life may be very erratically compassionate or even cruel.

Rinpoche: Yes, that is why—because it is below, it is at a deeper level.

Going into sleep

Student: Recently I've been noticing times just before you fall asleep and sometimes just when you wake up—it is like you're falling asleep and then you wake up again and your perception is totally different. It can sometimes be a bit scary—I am sure a lot of people experience this, it is difficult to put into words. I was wondering if it is possible there is some small, small insight into impermanence here? Because very often there is a sense of death; maybe like you were saying before, you're always dying?

Rinpoche: No, when I said that, it was a different thing. When you understand the totally impermanent nature of things very clearly and deeply, you don't necessarily have to feel insecure. You feel insecure when you are expecting to be secure. I think these kind of things that you are talking about can be because of many different reasons. But fear is always there. Everybody has lots of fear and everybody also has lots of different kinds of traumas at different levels. Sometimes we have this at the time of sleeping, when there can be experiences of many different levels.

I can't say exactly what is happening here, but the teaching and the practice are to try to put your mind as much as possible onto something positive when you go to sleep. You can visualise enlightened beings, feel the blessings and transformed state of mind as much as possible.

Then visualise light radiating from your heart and try to go to sleep in that positive way. This is said to be one way of going into sleep without the interruption of habitual tendencies. It breaks that habit. But these experiences can come from many different things.

Being like a river

Student: With regard to our individuality and the constantly changing river that flows, I was wondering about how I seem to have a continuity of consciousness through memory since I was a baby. Similarly, although the Thames, for example, is constantly changing, it is not the same as the Nile or the Euphrates or the Ganges. Can you say something about that? Is that purely to do with place? Or is there something more essential to do with something that is never born and can therefore never die?

Rinpoche: Yes, it is similar in a way. I, my mind, my experience—each moment of my experience—gives birth to the next moment of my experience. And the next moment of my experience gives birth to the *next* moment of my experience. That is the basis of continuation and the basis of rebirth; the basis of a continuum. The understanding from the Buddhist point of view is that this moment of my consciousness is not exactly the next moment of my consciousness, but without this moment of consciousness, the next moment of consciousness cannot happen. In that way, each moment of consciousness takes place. This life and the next life happen in the same way. This is the way in which change takes place, the continuum takes place. It is not something totally different. And it is not something totally continuing.

This is why there is the example, in the Abhidharmakosha, of milk turning into yoghurt: Milk is not yoghurt and yoghurt is not milk. But without milk there would be no yoghurt. When it is milk, it is not yoghurt. When it is yoghurt, it is not milk. When milk turns to yoghurt, milk is not there anymore. Where did the milk go? It did not go anywhere. The yoghurt in a way is the same thing. But it is not the same thing. This is the understanding of impermanence. This is the understanding of transformation. This is the understanding of continuum. So, your mind when you were a child is not the same as it is now, but without it your mind would not be here now. Not only your mind, but the whole thing. In the same way, according to the Buddhist way of seeing it, your past life and your future life are also not the same thing, but at the same time are not totally different.

Remaining open

Student: Can I ask a question about the difficulty of remaining open. It seems I close up so quickly and it is so easy to bring my habitual tendencies to my meditation practice. I would like to stay more open and fresh.

Rinpoche: Yes, that is very difficult. It is never said that it is easy—because it is not easy. But it is not impossible. That is the whole point. We have so many habitual tendencies to act or react in the way we do now. I talked about the way our mind is focused on problems. There are so many things happening in our day, though, it is possible if we choose, if we really develop the habit, we could focus our mind on something more positive and feel good, almost any time. But it is not easy because of our habitual tendencies. That is why training is necessary. That is why practice is necessary. And practice is all about this. We are not used to reacting in a certain way. We are not used to feeling openness and all these positive things. We need to make a conscious effort, but in a relaxed way, in a natural way, not beating ourselves up about it. That is skilful means. That is the meditation. We have to change these habitual tendencies.

We can't just say: 'Do it! Otherwise I'll beat you!' That would not work. We have to do it a certain way: give it some relaxation, give it some long rope, give it some good incentives, and encouragement. But then, persistently, with mindfulness, awareness, step by step, little by little, very slowly, develop this habit or ability. That is what we call practice. If I were able to do everything just like that, there would be no need to practice. Because we cannot do that, that is why practice is necessary. From the Buddhist point of view, the whole approach is seen as a training. Everything is seen as a training in how to train our mind, to transform. Actually Buddhism is not a belief system. It is not a culture. It is not a tradition. It is just a training system in how to train our mind to experience in a way that is better for us.

Responsibility

Student: Rinpoche, I found it really helpful the way that you describe the many causes and conditions. One of the things I realise I get caught up in is a feeling of responsibility. I realise of course I am not responsible but I feel a burden like I am responsible and I have to do something. When I heard you speak about the many causes and conditions it helped me to put myself in a huge context where I am a tiny, tiny part, which kind of frees something up. Then, putting that with the knowledge that I can make a difference, even in a very small way, it helps me to feel that I don't have to work hard to help somebody. I could do something quite small and that could actually have quite a significant effect.

Somebody once told me, I don't know if it's true, that when a NASA spacecraft is going to the moon, 97% of the time it is not on target. It is because it is continually righting itself that it gets there. There's something about that that just feels easier to put into action.

I wondered what you think about this feeling of being responsible?

Rinpoche: I think there are two things here. I think we are responsible for ourselves. How I react and how I experience is very much to do with myself. Of course there are lots of factors. I have very strong habits and habitual traditions; I have very strong addictions; I have very strong problems and things like that. But, it is all me—yes? So I have the responsibility. If anybody can do something about me, it is me. Nobody else can do anything about how I react, how I look at things, how I see things, nor where my mind is focused. It is only me that can do something. Nobody else can do it. So I am responsible. But it is not that I want to do something and it happens. For example: 'I don't want to focus my mind on negative things, only on positive things.' It doesn't happen just like that, does it? Because the way I am now is because of all the past. I cannot change everything just like that. I have to be patient. But I have to do it myself. So I have to know; I have to be responsible.

What happens to others because of me, or what happens with things because of my actions, there of course, I am one element. What I do has an effect, but how much effect it has, or in what way it will have that effect, depends on so many elements. So, therefore, if I want to do something good, it is not always necessary that it happens exactly as I wish it to happen. I can do only my best, nothing more than that. And then, whether I like it or not, I have to let go, let be. Sometimes it happens better than I expected. Sometimes it happens worse. And sometimes it happens totally shockingly. But what to do? That is how it happens. So if I expect too much, I get burnt out, thinking: 'It has to be like this ...' But it does not always happen like I want it to. The only thing that happens then is I get totally burnt out. That does not mean that I should not do things, but I should not worry too much, because worrying does not work either. I understand it like this.

Thank you very much.

It is a pleasure to be a student

I am a student.
I have been a student as long as I remember
And it is a pleasure to be a student.

It is a pleasure to learn that I don't know.
It is a pleasure to learn that I already know.
It is a pleasure to learn that I was mistaken.

It is a joy to learn from Great Masters.
It is a joy to learn by sharing what I learnt.
It is a joy to learn how to be what I am.

I seek to learn about the world around me.
I seek to learn about what I actually am.
I seek to learn how to be a proper human being.

Clouds show me the nature of my world.
Rivers show me the nature of myself.
Babies show me how to be more human.

I am a student.
I will be a student as long as I live.
And it is a pleasure to be a student.

Ringu Tulku Rinpoche

Mahamudra & Dzogchen

Ringu Tulku Rinpoche

Patrul Rinpoche's Dzogchen Centre, Brussels
29th July 2000

What is Mahamudra?

Mahamudra is the main practice or the ultimate practice of the Kagyu school of Tibetan Buddhism. However, it is taught not only in the Kagyu school but also in the Nyingma school. Mahamudra is the ultimate completion stage, the ultimate view and practice of the Anuttarayoga Tantra.

The Buddha's teachings can broadly be divided into two main sections:

1. The Sutrayâna, which encompasses the Mahâyâna and the Hinayâna;
and
2. The Vajrayâna, which is based on the Tantras.

The Tantras are sometimes classified into six, seven or nine classes, but generally, one considers four classes of Tantra, namely Kriya, Charya, Yoga and Anuttarayoga. The latter is the deepest, the highest class of Tantras. Tantras are also sometimes presented in four 'mudras', in which case the 'Mahamudra' is the culmination.

One important thing to remember is that Mahamudra has not just to do with the Kagyu. It is linked to the highest view, the highest experience, the ways and means to experience the true nature of ourselves.

As we all know, Buddhism is mainly a way to solve the problem of the sufferings of beings, to find a way out of these sufferings in a more ultimate way. From the Buddhist point of view, the basic cause or source of human beings' suffering is ignorance. From this ignorance come aversion and attachment. Ignorance, attachment and aversion are the three main causes of the sufferings of beings and of the samsaric state of mind.

Aversion and attachment are the ways we react at a subtle level. We categorize everything we see as either good/nice or bad/unpleasant. And then we react. We run after what we consider as good and run away from what we consider as bad. We can call this process 'fear' in a way. Attachment and aversion are regarded as two sides of the same coin. As long as we react in this way, we cannot get total peace and relaxation, joy and happiness.

Where do aversion and attachment come from? They come from ignorance, and what the Buddhist terminology defines as 'ignorance' which is seeing 'myself' as an independent entity, which is separate from everything else. I put 'myself' on one side, and everything else on the other side. It's 'I' versus 'the others'. When we have this basic attitude, all the experiences we have through our five senses are immediately categorized as something 'for' or 'against' me, and this gives rise to attachment and aversion. This sense of a separate identity is the basic problem. This seeing oneself as a separate entity is what we call 'co-emergent ignorance'.

What will really liberate us from these compulsive reactions which we call the 'samsaric state of mind', is to experience clearly, unmistakably and directly the way we really are, the true nature of ourselves and of all things. That is basically the objective of all Buddhist practices and of meditation.

The entire Buddhist Path is an inner search – or research – to discover our true nature. We have to find out what it is in an all-encompassing way, not just at an intellectual level. What we call sometimes 'Thatness', the 'nature of mind' or 'transcendental wisdom', is nothing other than the way things really are. It should be clear to everybody that Dharma practice should not be based on any belief or any dogma. It is an inner and honest search to find out through our own experience the way we really are. That is the main thrust of the practice.

There are many different teachings on how to do this. In a way, any teaching is one way or another way of working on the nature of the mind. Everything is either leading to that or directly talking about it. All the teachings are converging towards that point, because that is what really liberates us. As long as we don't clear away ignorance, as long as we are mistaken about who we are, we will remain in the samsaric state of mind and there will be no end to our suffering. Of course, we will experience moments of happiness, there will be good times, but as long as we have not cut the root of suffering, it will always be there.

Ground, Path and Result

This is also sometimes called the 'View', because it is an understanding, it is 'seeing' in an experiential way. But it's not only a View; it is also a Path and a Result.

Padmasambhava (Guru Rinpoche) said that the Ground is 'Uma', the Madhyamika; the Path is the 'cha dja chenpo', the Mahamudra; and the Result is 'Dzogpa Chenpo'. The Madhyamika is the main Buddhist philosophy that underlies the Mahayâna and the Vajrayâna. It is based on the Sutras, mainly the Prajnâpâramitâ Sutras and was propounded by Nâgârjuna and other great masters.

We call it the 'Ground', because that is where we study, where we learn. In the Buddhist way, we start by asking questions about everything. We proceed to an analysis. This is a very honest way of examining how we see things and how they really are, how much consistency there is between what our perceptions and our reasoning tell us. It's a little like science: we keep on asking questions, we use logic, reasoning, analysis to go deeper and see the contradictions between the way we perceive things and the result of our intellectual analysis. This leads us to a deeper understanding and we can therefore go down to the true nature of things. We try to go as far as our intellectual understanding can lead us and then we have to make a qualitative shift to an experiential understanding which transcends the intellect.

The 'Result' is Dzogchen. Dzogchen uses transcendental wisdom as the Path. We usually say that Vajrayâna as a whole uses the result as the path, but in the case of Dzogchen, it is not only the result but transcendental wisdom itself which is used as the Path. Dzogpa Chenpo is regarded as the profoundest teaching, because you are not only using the 'mind', but using 'rigpa'. Mind here stands for the deluded, samsaric state of mind, whereas rigpa is the clear mind, sometimes called the mind of clear light, which is beyond the samsaric state of mind. In Dzogchen, rigpa is used as a path right from the beginning. It is the most profound but not the easiest!

And then the 'Path' is Mahamudra. Here, the deluded mind is used as the path. Although it is basically about the same experience as Dzogchen, it starts with the deluded mind, with *shiné* and *lhakthong*. If we consider Mahamudra as the culmination point or ultimate view of the Anuttarayoga Tantra, then there is no real difference between Mahamudra and Dzogpa Chenpo. But when we use it as a Path, there is a difference. The Kagyu tradition has adopted the Mahamudra as a total path, by bringing the Sutrayāna teachings into it, mainly through incorporating the Five Treatises of Asanga/Maitreya, and especially the *Uttaratantra Shastra* or *Gyu Lama*. However, whichever tradition you are talking about, the objective remains to get to our most fundamental nature.

Mahamudra as a Path in the Kagyu tradition

In the Buddhist approach, you don't start from one point to get to your goal in a linear way. You take what you are as the basis and through different ways and means, you work to actualize what you really are. That is the Path. And what we find out by following the path is the Result. But it is difficult! We are enmeshed in so many different concepts and habits and habitual tendencies, all entangled one with the other, so it is difficult to find out what we really are. The first thing to do is to try and be natural. By 'natural', I don't mean our habitual way of reacting but our true, pristine nature. This is a process of de-conditioning. Karma and habitual patterns of reaction strongly condition us and we need to get slowly out of this strong conditioning, through meditation. This is why we start with *shiné*, proceed with *lhakthong* and then Mahamudra.

The Preliminaries

But before all that, we have the Ngöndro, the preliminary practices. These preliminaries are different ways to work on our various strong concepts: the way we grab at things, the way we see them as very solid, very real, very true. We progressively dismantle this way of seeing, first by an intellectual analysis that helps us understand how interdependent, compounded and impermanent things are, then by experiencing it. It is one thing to intellectualise, another to really experience it, and this is where meditation and visualizations come in.

Generally, in the tradition we follow, there is a set of preliminaries that are required prior to receiving the Mahamudra teachings. These preliminaries are there to help us work on certain experiences and reactions, on our way of seeing things. But it is not absolutely necessary to do it only in this way. The tradition says that unless you go through these preliminaries, you may not receive the actual teachings, but there is a problem there. We need to understand what we do for the preliminaries to work. If we don't understand what we are doing, if we don't connect, it won't work! If you do it only because you have been told you should do it, in a mechanical, formal way and without understanding why you do it, it is useless. It is therefore important to receive teachings so that you at least get a basic understanding of what it is for. With this understanding, you can connect with the practice.

In the first place, you should understand that the objective of Mahamudra is not to help you to feel a little better, to get a little calmer. What you are aiming at with Mahamudra is to liberate yourself completely from the samsaric state of mind, from the very cause of all your fears. I always call it 'fear' because I feel that fear is something very fundamental. Aversion comes out of fear; we dislike what might harm us. Attachment comes out of fear; we run after what we think we cannot do without, otherwise something terrible might happen to us.

Sometimes people think that fear is very useful, that without fear we would have no sense of danger and might run into trouble. Because we have always been in a samsaric state of mind, we don't know what it would actually be like to live without fear. However, the great masters tell us that we don't need to react only with a defence mechanism of fear in order to preserve our life. Actually, this defence mechanism is not the best way to react because it is reacting out of panic. There is another approach. If we don't panic, when we have no fear, we can see the situation more clearly and use our wisdom to decide what the best action would be.

The first thing we have to understand is that the possibility of liberation exists. Then we have a strong understanding of what the practice is all about. It is not something far away. Even enlightenment is no longer many lifetimes away, we can see the result now! And even if we are not the greatest of practitioners, we can at least understand it now. The instructions you receive from a teacher, like the 'pointing out instructions', are important, but a teacher can only point at things; one can never be sure the student will get what he means. He may look at the finger, or somewhere else. He has to understand on his own.

The introduction to Mahamudra is not given easily, not because there would be some copyright and you have to pay the right fee first, or because there is something secret about it, but simply because it is useless to give it to people who are not prepared to receive it. Actually, most teachers talk about it, but it goes by unnoticed. A preparation is needed and this is where the Ngöndro may be helpful. However, sometimes it isn't useful. Even if you do it all, it is not a guarantee that you are prepared. How much you are prepared depends on how much you have understood, how much you have changed.

And then, it is important to listen to the instructions again and again. I once attended a teaching by Nyoshul Ken Rinpoche. I went to see him to ask questions. He asked me whether I had already memorized the text, and when I admitted I had not, he said: 'First, you learn the text by heart, then you come back to me.' In order to remember a text, you have to read it many times, which helps you understand it. Memorising is a learning process. At first, you think you know what it means, but actually you know only the words. However, when you have all the information to hand, whenever something happens, you read something, get different instructions or some incident takes place, you immediately link it with the words, with the information you have memorised, and you get a deeper understanding. As what we are talking about is experiential, it is not only words.

This is illustrated by the story of Naropa and Tilopa. Naropa was a very learned, very famous professor at Nalanda University. He was very satisfied with himself. He used to think, 'People think I know a lot, but to tell the truth, I know everything.' But once, while he was reading a very deep treatise on tantra, and congratulating himself on how well he understood it, a shadow fell on his book and when he looked up, he saw an old woman. She said: 'You think you know, but actually you don't understand anything! You know only the words!' Naropa immediately understood that she was right and asked her: 'Who knows? ' When he heard her answer: 'My brother, Tilopa, he knows!' he didn't even bother to roll up his text, he stood up and left everything behind to go and search for Tilopa. He followed Tilopa for many years and during all these years, he went through terrible hardships imposed by Tilopa. He never received any formal teachings from Tilopa but he had an unshakable faith in him. And once, Tilopa got very angry – his behaviour was very unconventional and he used to flare up very readily in anger – and he threw his wooden sandal straight at Naropa's face. Naropa fainted, but when he came to, he knew everything that Tilopa knew! He had realized the true nature of everything.

This story illustrates the fact that this understanding is an experience. You may learn a lot, but it is still not enough.

The Four Yogas of Mahamudra

Mahamudra is usually taught in four stages:

- One-Pointedness
- Simplicity
- One Taste
- No-Meditation.

One-Pointedness

Regarding one-pointedness, Patrul Rinpoche said that we should start with cutting the movement of the mind. It is like *shiné*. We cut off the movement; we try not to follow the arisings, the perceptions of the five senses, the thoughts and emotions. We let the mind become less turbulent, calm down, abide in calm, rest and relax. This is working on our reactions: we stop hooking on to things. Aversion and attachment arise because, at a subtle level, we are hooking on to perceptions and then building on them. If we learn how not to hook on to whatever arises, we cut the 'following on' process and the chain reaction. Then our mind calms down and becomes clear and peaceful. That is the meditation we start with.

For instance, we concentrate on our breathing because breathing is happening all the time and it's happening now. Actually, by doing this, we are putting our mind in the very present moment. Thoughts and emotions are always connected to and based on past and future. We cannot follow thoughts if we stay in the present moment. For instance, if we make the statement 'this is good', we can say this because it is better than something we experienced in the past. Any reaction is always connected to our past experience. In the present moment, we simply 'are', without building upon anything and our mind then becomes naturally calm and therefore joyful. That is the state of *shiné* and it is the first part of one-pointedness.

The second part is, in a way, more important. It is all about experiencing stability within movement. It is not only when you are sitting, meditating in a calm place, that you can practise one-pointedness. Of course, this is very important and you can go very far through *shiné* meditation. You can attain complete control over your mind and body. You can let your mind be wherever you want and therefore, you have total control over the reactions of your body. That is what we call *'shin jang'* in Tibetan.

I think most people know the chart of the taming of the elephant. The first image shows an elephant, black, crazy and powerful, led by a monkey. A man with a small hook and a rope runs after them. The elephant represents our mind at the start. The crazy monkey jumping everywhere symbolizes the five senses and the man trying to catch the elephant is ourselves trying to tame our mind with the tools of awareness and vigilance. It seems at first a hopeless task, but slowly, slowly, we see the man catching up, putting the rope around the elephant's neck, sitting on his back, and leading him wherever he wants. The monkey disappears and the elephant gradually becomes white and tame, so tame that at the end there is no need of a rope and a hook. He sits quietly beside the man.

To tame our stubborn, violent and very active mind is not easy. It needs subtle handling and lots of persistence. We should be aware of our goal and be diligent, knowing at the same time that it is all about letting be. Usually, when we are motivated and diligent in doing anything it is in a tense way, but meditation is not 'doing' anything. It is letting things cool down, remaining in the primordially natural state. We have to find a balance between effort and relaxation. We should 'do' meditation in a way by 'not doing'. This can only be learned through experience. It is like everything you learn, driving a car for instance. The theory is easy to learn. It took me one day to pass the examination, but it took me three months to really know how to drive and I failed the test twice before passing. You can have the best teachers, as I did, and they can tell you everything you have to do, which is certainly very useful, but then you have to do it yourself. The theory is one thing, practice is another!

But let's go back to the second part. Stability in meditation is important, but the main thing is to learn how to be stable within the movement of the mind. That's the very important part. If you can find that, then nothing can disturb you any longer. The stability you can experience by cutting off the movement can be lost. If something happens, if a strong disturbance arises, you will lose it. The stability you experience within the movement, when the mind and the five senses are functioning, when thoughts and emotions are going on, that stability is what we call the real one-pointedness. It's in a way an extension of the first one, but it goes much deeper. Thoughts and emotions are arising all the time. You should see them as a part of the mind; as its radiance, like the radiance of the sun. When you perceive it like that, there is no need to fear these arisings any more; you can just let them be!

Many people know the story of Lady Paldarbum and Milarepa. Milarepa gave these instructions to her : 'Meditate like the sky, without centre or limits. Meditate like the sea, without bottom. Meditate like the mountain, with stability.' Then, having meditated for a while, Lady Paldarbum came to see Milarepa and she asked him: 'It's very nice to meditate like the sky, but what do I do when there are clouds passing in the sky? It's very good to meditate like the sea, but what about the waves? It's very well to meditate when my mind is calm and clear, but what should I do when thoughts and emotions arise?' Then Milarepa told her: 'The clouds in the sky do not bother the sky; they come and go without changing its nature. The waves are no problem to the sea, as they are simply part of the sea. It is the same for your mind. Thoughts and emotions should not bother you, as they are part of your mind; they are just its natural manifestation.'

It's all a question of taking whatever arises as a part of the mind. It comes and goes without disturbing you. Joy, sadness, anger, desire, insecurity, all the thoughts and emotions just come and go. It's okay. When you know that whatever comes will go anyway, you can let it come, you are no longer overpowered by what arises. And then you have real confidence. You know that you can handle whatever comes, you have nothing to fear. Everything is okay. A strong and complete experience of that is one-pointedness, and it can go a long way. When we talk about Mahamudra, we can talk about these four stages but even if only the first part can be experienced, it is almost enough.

Simplicity

The second point is usually translated as 'simplicity'. It is more like *lhakthong*, that is, finding our true nature. Patrul Rinpoche describes it as follows :

> 'Through looking at or analysing relative truth, find ultimate truth. By examining ultimate truth, see how relative truth arises'.

It is all about understanding deeply the nature of the two truths and seeing that they are not two different things. When we see this clearly, we understand the union of appearances and emptiness. This analysis differs from the scientific approach in that scientists look 'out', whereas in Buddhist practice, we look out but also 'in'. We have the experience of finding emptiness and selflessness, the inseparability of awareness and emptiness; of appearances and emptiness. Going beyond any opposite extremes like these is the experience of simplicity.

One Taste

This leads to the next point, 'one taste'. It's the experience of going beyond *samsâra* and *nirvâna*. *Samsâra* and *nirvâna* are just concepts. They are not two things, they are the same thing; it is just a question of a different perception. *Samsâra* is what we perceive with a temporary distortion whereas *nirvâna* is what we perceive when this distortion has been cleared. A profound experience of the two truths as being one is what we call one taste. When we realize this, we no longer react with aversion, fear or attachment. It is not an experience of indifference but of complete clarity. Everything is extremely clear. In its essence, our mind is clarity or clear awareness. There is no barrier; it is unlimited, and therefore we can see everything. It is only when we are conditioned that we limit ourselves and do not use the full capacity of our mind. When we understand the unlimited character of our mind, we no longer say 'I' or 'me'. The Buddha never said 'I'; he always referred to himself as the '*Tathâgata*', which means 'thus gone' or 'thus come', an indication that he is not the first or last Buddha, he just found what is there. This experience is what we call one taste.

No Meditation

The last stage is called 'no meditation'. It is almost like the result, the ultimate stage of Mahamudra. Even one taste becomes fully matured and we experience that there is nothing more to do, no more to work on, no *samsâra* to be abandoned and no *nirvâna* to be attained. We realize that enlightenment has always been there; it is not even something that we have developed or just realized.

So these are the four stages of Mahamudra, and I think that is all I can say about it. For those who practise Mahamudra, the first stage is the most important. Although analysis is not done in Mahamudra exactly like in the Madhyamika, the understanding of Madhyamika philosophy is also important. Those who practise Mahamudra should also obtain an understanding of the type of analysis used in Madhyamika.

Guru Yoga and devotion

We usually practise Mahamudra within Guru Yoga. This is also the case with Dzogchen which is practised in the context of Guru Yoga.

It is important to understand that there are two Buddhist approaches. On the one hand, Buddhism is very rational. We should not accept anything blindly. Even the Buddha said that we should examine his words and only accept them when we come to a personal conclusion that they are good and true. There is a strong emphasis on logic in Buddhism and it has a rational basis. On the other hand, Buddhism also uses less rational approaches. It is the case with devotion, which is used as a strong medium of practice.

The devotion to the Buddha, to a guru or a yidam is used as a path (and it is a very strong path), especially in the Mahamudra teachings, where you have to go beyond the intellect. We use devotion because devotion is a clear and positive emotion and a strong medium of meditation. We should understand what we are talking about here. This is different from being devoted to a person. Of course, you can be devoted to someone, but here we are talking more about devotion in itself, devotion as a 'path'. It is not the object of the devotion that is important, it is the devotion itself which possesses a great strength and, in a way, makes the miracle happen.

There is the story of the dog's tooth. There was a Tibetan merchant who regularly travelled to India for his business. His mother was very devoted. The first time he left for India, she asked him to bring back some relics from the Buddha, as he was going to this very holy country, the very place where the Buddha had lived and taught. But the son forgot. The next time, his mother repeated her request, but the son forgot again. This happened several times. Then, the mother threatened her son: 'I am getting old and I may die soon. Now, this time you are going, if you don't bring me back some relic from the Buddha, I will kill myself in front of you!' But once again, the son forgot. However, on his way back, he remembered his mother's words. You know, Tibetans are very stubborn, and he knew that his mother was perfectly capable of doing what she had promised and killing herself in front of him. He was not very far from his village and he looked around to find something. Then he saw the skeleton of a dog. He took off one of its teeth, cleaned it, polished it a little bit and wrapped it in beautiful Indian silk. When he arrived home, he gave it to his mother, saying: 'This time, I brought back your relic, and what a relic! The very tooth of the Buddha himself!' His mother wept with joy and put the dog's tooth on her altar. She would pray and pray all day long with the deepest devotion. After a while, rainbows and five-coloured rays started shining from the tooth and when the old woman died, many wonderful signs were seen.

Of course, the object of our devotion may have its importance also, but we should understand that the emphasis is on the devotion itself and this is why these practices are usually done within the context of guru yoga.

Questions and discussion

Student: You said that fear is at the core of attachment and aversion, is it also at the core of ignorance?

Rinpoche: No, ignorance is at the core of fear.

Student: You mentioned the 'clear mind', I understood that there is something behind the mind, is it correct?

Rinpoche: You can say that. And you can also say it is not correct. The conscious mind has different levels. From the point of view of Mahamudra, we talk about a co-emergent wisdom and a co-emergent ignorance. The co-emergent ignorance is our experience of an ego, the distorted, wrong perception of ourselves. The co-emergent wisdom is the way we experience ourselves and the world as it is, when that misunderstanding has been cleared. 'Co-emergent' is used because it is always there; therefore it is not 'behind' in a way. You can say 'behind' in the sense that our perceptions are clouded by our conditioning.

Student: What do you mean by 'getting connected' in the context of practice?

Rinpoche: Understanding, knowing the reasons underlying the practice, how it is working. To connect with the practice, we have to know how it might help us, otherwise it remains formal, exterior to us and we will have doubts as to the use of what we are doing. We should first have an idea of the direction we take and know why we are practicing. I believe that we should first learn how to practice, how the practice works, why we do it, and then only do it. You should only practice what you understand. The most suitable practice is a practice that you understand. When you know what you are doing and why you are doing it, it is easy to practice. When you feel it is easy, you will practice it, and then you will get results.

Student: I have been taught that the fact of being separated from the other people is an illusion. I would like to know then, when we die and are reborn, is it truly 'me'?

Rinpoche: 'Separate' may not be the right word. In Buddhism, you look at something, anything, and you ask what it is made of. What am I? Am I one thing or many things? When you investigate something, it is not advisable to jump directly to the conclusions, but when we are teaching like this, this is the only way we can talk about it due to the lack of time. We come to the conclusion that the body is made of many elements and that the mind is also a composite thing that is changing all the time. One thought is not the next, all experiences are different. Moreover, our concepts and perceptions are linked to many things, it is interdependent. We cannot find in ourselves any independent, permanent thing that we can define as 'I'. Like everything else, we are a continuum. However, we feel that we are one independent thing. As I just explained, we perceive ourselves as 'me' opposed to all the 'others. Of course, I am not my neighbour. But I am not one thing either.

We are liberated from fear when we realise that there is nothing existing from its own side that we can secure in ourselves, so in a way, we have no need of security. And moreover, there is nothing that can be destroyed. Therefore, there is nothing to reincarnate.

The Buddhist way of seeing reincarnation differs from the Hindu. Hindus view reincarnation just like changing clothes. Very broadly speaking, we could say that it is also the Buddhist approach, but when we consider things more deeply, or read the Abhidharmakosha for instance, it is clear that it is not the case. It is only a continuum. My next life is not exactly me and is not exactly not me. One moment of 'me' is caused by the last moment of me and the reactions I had. And the same moment is also the cause of the next moment. So it's not only life after life, but moment by moment. This change is constant. I'm not the same person I was an hour ago, but I'm not a different person either. The classical examples are: recitation, a flame, a mirror, a seal and yoghurt.

When I recite something and you remember it, how does this transfer take place? Is the flame of a candle the same at the beginning and at the end of the burning process? The reflection of yourself in a mirror is not you, but it would not be there if you did not stand in front of the mirror. The imprint of the seal would also not be there without the seal. As to the yoghurt, it is not milk. When you have milk, you don't have yoghurt, when you have yoghurt, you no longer have milk, but you cannot have yoghurt without milk. Things exist in this way, they are a little mysterious.

Dedication

All my babbling,
In the name of Dharma
Has been set down faithfully
By my dear students of pure vision.

I pray that at least a fraction of the wisdom
Of those enlightened teachers
Who tirelessly trained me
Shines through this mass of incoherence.

May the sincere efforts of all those
Who have worked tirelessly
Result in spreading the true meaning of Dharma
To all who are inspired to know.

May this help dispel the darkness of ignorance
In the minds of all living beings
And lead them to complete realisation
Free from all fear.

Ringu Tulku

Glossary and Notes

Abhidharmakosha (Sanskrit; Tibetan *ngön pa dzod*) An authoritative scripture on Buddhist metaphysics according to the Hinayana tradition. It is otherwise known as 'The Compendium of Abhidharma' or 'The Treasure House of Knowledge', and is a text written by Vasubandhu (*circa* 4th century CE), which concerns the difference between the phenomena of *samsara* (see below) and those of *nirvana* (see below).

Afflictive emotions are the negative emotions or *kleshas* (see below) of grasping or attachment, aversion or aggression, and ignorance. The afflictive emotions may be given different names, in different classification systems (e.g. passion, hatred, delusion) and also include pride, jealousy and other negative mental states.

Anatman (Sanskrit) refers to the non-existence of the 'I' or 'self', so it is often translated as non-self.

Anuttarayoga Tantra (Tibetan *nal jor la na me pay ju*) There are four levels of the Vajrayana and Anuttarayoga tantra is the highest of these. It includes the Guhyasamaja, the Chakrasamvara, the Hevajra and the Kalachakra tantras.

Asanga (Tibetan *thok may*) A fourth century Indian philosopher who founded the Cittamatra or Yogacara school and wrote the five works of Maitreya which are important Mahayana works.

Bardo (Tibetan) The intermediate state between the end of one life and rebirth into another. Bardo can also be divided into six different levels; the bardo of birth, dreams, meditation, the moment before death, the bardo of dharmata (the true nature of reality), and the bardo of becoming.

Channels refers to the *'channels'* of the subtle body, known as *nadi* (Sanskrit) or *tsa* (Tibetan), through which the subtle energies and essences flow. There are three major subtle channels in the body: the right, left, and central channel. These channels are not anatomical ones but conduits through which subtle energy flows.

Charya Yoga Tantra is one of the four classes of tantra. It is known as the 'conduct' tantra because it emphasises outer actions of the body and speech as well as meditative absorption of the mind.

Dependent arising (Tibetan: *rten cing brel bar byung ba*), or (inter)dependent origination or interdependence, refers to the arising of samsaric phenomena.

Dzogchen and **Dzogpa Chenpo** (Sanskrit *mahasandhi*) Literally 'the great perfection' The teachings beyond the vehicles of causation, first taught in the human world by Garab Dorje.

Emptiness or *shunyata* (Sanskrit; Tibetan *tong pa nyi*). As Ringu Tulku says in this teaching: '*Emptiness does not mean there is nothing, emptiness means the way everything is, the way everything magically manifests*'. Sometimes also translated as voidness. The Buddha taught in the second turning of the wheel of dharma that external phenomena and the internal phenomena or concept of self or 'I' have no real existence and therefore are 'empty.' It is a term indicating the lack of any truly existing independent nature of any and all phenomena.

Five Treatises of Asanga are texts said to have been related to Asanga by the Buddha Maitreya and are central to the 'Mind Only' (Yogacara or Cittamatra) school of Buddhist philosophy.

Guru Rinpoche see **Padmasambhava**

Guru Yoga (Tib. *lamay naljor*) A practice of devotion to the guru culminating in receiving his blessing and blending indivisibly with his mind.

Habitual tendencies refers to the propensities to act or react in certain ways produced by past actions.

Heart Sutra (*Sanskrit Mahaprajnaparamita-hridaya-sutra*) is a short rendition of the Perfection of Wisdom (*Prajnaparamita*, see below) Buddhist texts.

Hinayana Buddhism (Tibetan *tek pa chung wa*) Literally, the 'lesser vehicle.' The first of the three yanas, or vehicles. The term refers to the first teachings of the Buddha, which emphasized the careful examination of mind and its confusion. It is the foundation of Buddha's teachings, focusing mainly on the Four Noble Truths and the twelve interdependent links of origination.

Humours are the balance of fluids (black bile, yellow bile, phlegm and blood) in the human body, which control health and emotion, according to ancient Greek and Roman medicine. Also in Tibetan medicine: three humours: wind energy (Tib. *rlung*), bile energy (Tib. *mkhris pa*) and phlegm (Tib. *bad kan*).

Kagyu (Tibetan) *Ka* means oral and *gyu* means lineage; the lineage of oral transmission. One of the four major schools of Buddhism in Tibet. It was founded in Tibet by Marpa and is headed by His Holiness Karmapa. The other three are the Nyingma, the Sakya and the Gelugpa schools.

Karma (Sanskrit; Tibetan *lay*) refers to deeds and actions underlying the cycle of cause and effect; it is commonly used to refer to the consequences of those actions (*karma-phala* in Sanskrit).

Kleshas (Sanskrit *kleśa*; Tibetan *nyön mong*) refer to mental defilements, mind poisons or afflictive emotions (see above). They include any emotion that disturbs or distorts consciousness. The three main kleshas are desire, anger and ignorance. The five kleshas are the three above plus pride and envy/jealousy.

Kriya Yoga Tantra (Tibetan *ja way gyu*) One of the four tantras which emphasizes personal purity.

Lhathong (Tibetan) or '*vipassana*' (Pali; Sanskrit *vipaśyanā*) is 'insight' meditation, which is usually practised after gaining some experience of 'calm-abiding' meditation (*shiné* or *shamatha*). It refers to insight into emptiness.

Madhyamika (Tibetan *u ma*) is the most influential of the four schools of Indian Buddhism founded by Nagarjuna in the second century C.E. It is 'the Middle-way' between eternalism and nihilism. The main postulate of this school is that all phenomena (both internal mental events and external physical objects) are empty of any true nature.

Magical refers to the ephemeral and transitory way that phenomena can appear to the (realised) mind.

Mahamudra (Tibetan *cha ja chen po or phyag chen*) literally means 'great seal' or 'great symbol', meaning that all phenomena are 'sealed' by the primordially perfect true nature. Mahamudra is an advanced form of meditation practice, comprising methods of attaining a direct introduction to the nature and essence of the mind. It emphasizes perceiving mind directly rather than through rational analysis. It also refers to the experience of the practitioner where one attains the union of emptiness and luminosity and perceives the non-duality of the phenomenal world and emptiness.

Mahayana Buddhism (Sanskrit; Tibetan *tek pa chen po*) refers to one of the two main branches of Buddhism existing today, the other being Theravada Buddhism. The term *'Mahayana'* may be translated as *'Great Vehicle'* and relates to the Path of the Bodhisattva who vows to liberate all sentient beings from the sufferings of *samsara* (see below). These are the teachings of the second turning of the wheel of dharma, which emphasize *shunyata*, compassion and universal Buddha nature. The purpose of enlightenment is to liberate all sentient beings from suffering as well as oneself. Mahayana schools of philosophy appeared several hundred years after the Buddha's death, although the tradition is traced to a teaching he is said to have given at Rajagriha, or Vulture Peak Mountain.

Maitreya is 'The Loving One'; the bodhisattva regent of Buddha Shakyamuni, presently residing in the Tushita heaven until becoming the fifth Buddha of this degenerate age.

Milarepa lived in Tibet in the 11th-12th centuries CE and was a wandering yogi famous for his spontaneous songs of realisation. He is said to have attained complete enlightenment in one lifetime, after an inauspicious early career as a black magician, through the trials and teachings of his Guru, Marpa the Translator.

Nagarjuna (Tibetan *ludrup*) lived in India in the 2nd-3rd centuries CE and founded the Middle Way (Sanskrit: *Madhyamaka*) school of Buddhism. He is associated with the philosophy of *emptiness* as expressed in the *Prajnaparamita* Sutra.

Nature of the mind, as Ringu Tulku says in this teaching: *'the nature of mind is clarity'*. It is also taught to be inseparable from emptiness and compassionate energy in Mahayana Buddhism.

Ngöndro (Tibetan *sngon 'gro*): preliminary practices or foundational practices, the purpose of which is to clear our minds and allow practice to progress smoothly.

Nirvana (Sanskrit; *Tibetan nyangde*) literally means 'extinguished' and is the state of being free from suffering (see *samsara*).

Nyingma (Tibetan) is the oldest school of Buddhism based on the teachings of Padmasambhava and others in the eighth and ninth centuries.

Nyoshul Khen Rinpoche (1932-1999) was a great Tibetan Dzogchen master.

Padmasambhava (Guru Rinpoche), known as the 'Lotus Born' is the great 8th century Indian mahasiddha who came to Tibet to tame all the negative elemental forces and spread the Buddhadharma. In particular he taught many tantras and Vajrayana practices, and concealed many texts to be later revealed by his disciples.

Paldarbum or *Nyama Paldarbum* was a female disciple of Milarepa, who practiced as a yogini in everyday life.

Paramita (Sanskrit) means *'perfection'*, *'transcendental'* or culmination of specific virtues, which are often given as the six of: generosity, moral ethics or discipline, patience, effort or diligence, meditative concentration and wisdom (which is *prajnaparamita* itself). The ten paramitas are the above six with: skilful means, aspiration, strength and primordial wisdom. When perfected, they are pure actions free from dualistic concepts.

Patrul Rinpoche (1808-1887) was a great Tibetan Dzogchen master, and author of *'The Words of My Perfect Teacher'*.

Prajna (Sanskrit; Tibetan *she rab*) means the *'wisdom'*, or *'perfect knowledge'* of seeing things from a non-dualistic point of view. In the Buddhist context, it is the wisdom of the direct realisation of the Four Noble Truths, impermanence, interdependence, karma, non-self and emptiness.

Prajnaparamita Sutra: the Perfection of Wisdom texts, or scriptural canon of Mahayana Buddhism (see above).

Rigpa is sometimes said not to be translatable as it relates to the realised mind. It may, however, perhaps be understood as 'self-reflexive awareness' i.e. awareness recognising itself as being aware.

Samsara/samsaric (Sanskrit; Tibetan *kor wa*) is the state of suffering (see *nirvana)* of 'cyclic existence.' It is the conditioned existence of ordinary life in which suffering occurs because, through the force of karma, there is attachment, aggression and ignorance.

Self refers to the 'True Self' in contrast to the ego or '*I*'. As Ringu Tulku says in this teaching: '...the more you understand emptiness and interdependence (whether you call it selflessness or *Self*), the more you know how to deal with your problems and your habitual tendencies'.

Selflessness (Tibetan *dag me*) relates to *anatman* (see above) or non-self, and also to altruism and egolessness.

Shiné (Tibetan *zhi gnas*) or **Shamatha** (Sanskrit *śamatha*) is calm abiding meditation; calming the mind.

Shin jang (Tibetan) means 'pliable mind'.

Shunyata or **sunyata** (Sanskrit): see *'emptiness'* above.

Sutrayana is the sutra approach to achieving enlightenment which includes both the Hinayana and the Mahayana.

Tantra (Tibetan *gyu*) literally means 'continuity,' and in Buddhism refers to both the texts and to the Tantric and Vajrayana meditative practices themselves.

Tathagata (Sanskrit) is the name the Buddha used to refer to himself in the Sutras, and it means both the 'One Thus Gone' and the 'One Thus Come'.

Uttaratantra Shastra (Sanskrit; Tibetan or *gyu lama*) is Asanga's crucial work on Buddha nature.

Vajrayana (Tibetan *dorje tek pa*) literally means 'diamond-like' or 'indestructible capacity.' The Vajrayana is based on the Tantras and is the method of taking the result as the path.

Yidam (Tibetan) is a tantric deity that embodies the qualities of Buddhahood and is meditated upon in the Vajrayana. *Yi* means mind and *dam* means pure or inseparable. Thus the yidam represents the practitioner's awakened nature or pure appearance.

Yoga Tantra is the class of tantra that emphasizes meditation upon reality, combining skilful means and wisdom.

Acknowledgments

I would like to take this opportunity to thank everyone involved in the publication of Heart Wisdom Four: Mary Heneghan and Jonathan Clewley for their hard work in transcribing and editing the Emptiness teaching. To Corinne Segars for the original transcript and edit of Mahamudra and Dzogchen. To Pat Little for helping me re-edit Mahamudra and Dzogchen. To the Bodhicharya Publications team, especially Tim Barrow, Rachel Moffit, Dave Tuffield, Eric Masterton, Pat Murphy and Jet Mort for their proof reading of this publication.

As always, to Paul O'Connor for layout and design and his unending patience.

With grateful thanks and love to Ringu Tulku for continuing to share his heart wisdom here.

Margaret Ford
Bodhicharya Publications
October 2011

About the Author

Ringu Tulku Rinpoche is a Tibetan Buddhist Master of the Kagyu Order. He was trained in all schools of Tibetan Buddhism under many great masters including HH the 16th Gyalwang Karmapa and HH Dilgo Khyentse Rinpoche. He took his formal education at Namgyal Institute of Tibetology, Sikkim and Sampurnananda Sanskrit University, Varanasi, India. He served as Tibetan Textbook Writer and Professor of Tibetan Studies in Sikkim for 25 years.

Since 1990, he has been travelling and teaching Buddhism and meditation in Europe, America, Canada, Australia and Asia. He participates in various interfaith and 'Science and Buddhism' dialogues and is the author of several books on Buddhist topics. These include *Path to Buddhahood, Daring Steps, The Ri-me Philosophy of Jamgon Kongtrul the Great, Confusion Arises as Wisdom*, the *Lazy Lama* series and the *Heart Wisdom* series, as well as several children's books, available in Tibetan and European languages.

He founded the organisations Bodhicharya - see www.bodhicharya.org and Rigul Trust - see www.rigultrust.org.

Other books by Ringu Tulku

ALSO PUBLISHED BY BODHICHARYA PUBLICATIONS:
THE LAZY LAMA SERIES.

- *Buddhist Meditation*
- *The Four Noble Truths*
- *Refuge: Finding a Purpose and a Path*
- *Bodhichitta: Awakening Compassion and Wisdom*
- *Living without Fear and Anger*

PUBLISHED BY SHAMBHALA:

- *Path to Buddhahood: Teachings on Gampopa's 'Jewel Ornament of Liberation'*
- *Daring Steps: Traversing the Path of the Buddha*
- *Mind Training*
- *The Ri-Me Philosophy of Jamgon Kongtrul the Great:*
  A Study of the Buddhist Lineages of Tibet.
- *Confusion Arises as Wisdom:*
  Gampopa's Heart Advice on the Path of Mahamudra.

PUBLISHED BY RIGUL TRUST:

Chenrezig: The Practice of Compassion
A Commentary

PUBLISHED BY FINDHORN PRESS:

The Boy who had a Dream
An illustrated book for children
Available from Rigul Trust at www.rigultrust.org

For an up to date list of books by Ringu Tulku, please see the Books section at

www.bodhicharya.org

All proceeds received by Bodhicharya Publications from the sale of this book go direct to humanitarian and educational projects because the work involved in producing this book has been given free of charge.